MODERN ERAS · UNCOVERED ·
the mid 1970s to the mid 1980s

From Punk Rock to Perestroika

Pat Levy

Raintree

www.raintreepublishers.co.uk
Visit our website to find out more information about **Raintree** books.

To order:
☎ Phone 44 (0) 1865 888113
▤ Send a fax to 44 (0) 1865 314091
▢ Visit the Raintree Bookshop at **www.raintreepublishers.co.uk** to browse our catalogue and order online.

First published in Great Britain by Raintree, Halley Court, Jordan Hill, Oxford, OX2 8EJ, part of Harcourt Education.
Raintree is a registered trademark of Harcourt Education Ltd.

© Harcourt Education Ltd 2006
The moral right of the proprietor has been asserted.

Editorial: Melanie Copland and Lucy Beevor
Design: Michelle Lisseter and
Bridge Creative Services Ltd
Picture Research: Mica Brancic and Ginny Stroud-Lewis
Production: Duncan Gilbert

Originated by Chroma Graphics (Overseas) Pte. Ltd
Printed and bound in China by South China Printing Company

ISBN 1 844 43956 9
10 09 08 07 06
10 9 8 7 6 5 4 3 2 1

British Library Cataloguing in Publication Data
Levy, Patricia
From Punk Rock to Perestroika. – (Modern Eras Uncovered)
909. 8'27

A full catalogue record for this book is available from the British Library.

Acknowledgements
Corbis pp. **43, 48**; Corbis/Alain Nogues p. **19**; Corbis/Bettmann pp. **9, 18, 21, 23, 26, 45, 35**; Corbis/Grant Smith p. **39**; Corbis/J L Atlan p. **47**; Corbis/Leif Skoogfors p. **33**; Corbis/Lynn Goldsmith p. **12**; Corbis/Neal Preston p. **37**; Corbis/Peter Russell; The Military Picture Library p. **24**; Corbis/ S.I.N. p. **34**; Corbis/Sygma/Arnold Cedric p. **29**; Corbis/Wally McNamee pp. **6, 32**; Getty Images pp. **13, 15**; Getty Images/AFP p. **17**; Getty Images Editorial /Tony Duffy p. **25**; Getty Images/Hulton Archives pp. **28, 41, 44**; Getty Images/PhotoDisc p. **16**; Getty Images/Time Life Pictures p. **27**; PA Photos p. **4**; Popperfoto p. **8**; Rex Features p. **31**; The Advertising Archives Ltd pp. **14, 46**; The Bridgeman Art Library (Private Collection) © ADAGP, Paris and DACS, London, 2004 p. **38**; The Historical Newspaper Loan Service p. **30**; The Kobal Collection/Lucas Films/20th Century Fox p. **5**; The Kobal Collection/Paramount p. **11**; The Kobal Collection/Spelling Goldberg p. **10**; The Kobal Collection/Universal pp. **49, 7**; Topfoto pp. **36, 40**.

Cover photograph (top) reproduced with permission of Getty Images/Paul Chesley Stone, and photograph (bottom) reproduced with permission of Corbis/Peter Turnley.

Every effort has been made to contact copyright holders of any material reproduced in this book. Any omissions will be rectified in subsequent printings if notice is given to the publishers.

The paper used to print this book comes from sustainable resources.

CONTENTS

Any words appearing in the text in bold, **like this**, are explained in the glossary.

HOPES AND FEARS

The late 1970s were troubled years. International problems that had been building up over the previous decades came to dominate world news. The war in Vietnam finally drew to a close after the withdrawal of US troops. In the **Middle East** the conflict between Israel and Arab countries spread. In Northern Ireland, violent conflict that went back to the division of the island around fifty years earlier became a regular item of news around the world.

This was also a time of unemployment and **economic recession** in Europe and the United States. Unemployed and angry young people started to rebel against society, which they felt had no use for them. Many joined the punk culture, which had started in the United States and spread across the UK and Europe.

For the first time, people began to have worries about modern technology. The weapons that were supposed to protect them might instead end up destroying the whole world in a nuclear war. The **Cold War**, the bad feeling between the United States and the **USSR**, became more hostile. Each side felt it was necessary to spend more money building up stockpiles of nuclear weapons.

A group of "punks," with colourful hair and make-up, gather in Brixton, London, for the "Rock the Bomb" festival of peace in May 1983.

People also became more aware that the environment was being damaged in many different ways. Some animal **species** were becoming extinct and habitats were being destroyed. **Natural resources** such as oil and gas, which fuelled modern life, were being used more and more, but no one knew how long these resources would last.

By the middle of the 1980s, the economic recession had ended. It was also a time when the two **superpowers**, the United States and USSR were prepared to talk to each another about how to avoid conflict. In the USSR the new leader, Mikhail Gorbachev, was telling the **West** that he wanted openness and reform and, above all, an end to the build up of nuclear weapons.

Star Wars

In 1977, the movie *Star Wars* told a thrilling tale with amazing special effects. For the first time in movie history, actors were asked to imagine some of the other characters, which were put in by special effects teams later. The actors in the movie were not famous at the time, as a lot of money had to be spent instead on the special effects. The story, unlike the reality of the Cold War, was a simple tale of good and evil that people could respond to.

This still shows the 1977 movie *Star Wars*, which made the then-unknown actors, especially Harrison Ford (right), into international stars.

The UK had joined the European Economic Community (later called the EU) in 1973, but by 1975 the UK was having difficulties. The government was in dispute with **trade unions** over wages, unemployment was rising and **inflation** was high. The Irish Republican Army (**IRA**) stepped up its campaign for independence from the UK, and carried out a series of bomb attacks. For the first time in UK history a woman, Margaret Thatcher, was elected leader of a UK political party.

Economic problems

Since the end of the Second World War the **economies** of the West had been steadily growing. Economists believed that there would never again be a **recession** like the one that had hit the whole world in the 1930s. Then, suddenly, in the early 1970s trade started to slow down, prices of basic goods rose, and demand for manufactured goods fell. In 1975, steel production in some countries fell by half. In the United States, New York City Council declared itself almost bankrupt and was unable to pay its employees. In Detroit, whose major industry was manufacturing cars, a quarter of all workers in car manufacturing lost their jobs.

No one knew for sure why this was happening. Some blamed it on the rise in oil prices in the early 1970s, making the cost of transport and manufacture higher, and so putting up prices.

The special relationship between the governments of the U.S. and United Kingdom was never stronger than in the 1980s. In 1975, and for the first time in UK history, a woman, Margaret Thatcher, was elected leader of a UK political party. By 1979, she had been elected prime minister. Throughout Thatcher's eleven-year term in office she and Ronald Reagan, who would be elected president of the U.S. in 1980, remained close friends and **allies**. The two leaders forged a connection which dominated the international scene for a decade.

In **developing countries** that depended on the sale of raw materials such as wood, coal, or mined metals, the recession was even worse. Sales fell and the cost of transport rose. In these countries there was less government support for the unemployed than in the West and so people were more badly affected by the recession.

Changing times

The effect of the recession on people's confidence was enormous. For the first time, people began to realize that the world's oil might one day run out. Some people began to wonder if the modern technology they were all depending on might one day harm the environment. In some parts of the world especially hard hit by the recession, such as Africa, leaders began to question the fairness of a system where rich countries seemed to have become rich at the expense of poorer ones.

Jaws

If *Star Wars* offered an escape from troubled times, the 1975 film *Jaws* seemed to reflect people's sense of anxious times. The film told the story of a local sheriff's attempts to protect holidaymakers against a deadly great white shark. The music that led up to the appearances of the shark – a mechanical model that looked frighteningly real – was very menacing. The film made US$470 million worldwide in ticket sales. No film had ever made that much money. It was only the second feature film that Steven Spielberg had directed.

This is a frightening still from Steven Spielberg's 1975 movie, *Jaws*, regarded by many as one of his best movies.

Power struggles

Since the end of the Second World War the world's two superpowers, the United States and the USSR, had been against one another in what came to be known as the Cold War. Neither the United States nor the USSR actually fought each other. Instead, each tried to limit any influence the other country might have somewhere else in the world. This sometimes included sending weapons and even troops to a country and supporting a war that seemed to have little to do with people at home.

Vietnam

In Asia, Vietnam had been fighting wars since 1946. At first it waged a war of independence to free itself from the French **empire**. In 1954, Vietnam gained its independence, but a war developed between the divided north and south of the country. The United States believed that by supporting South Vietnam against the **communist** North they could stop other neighbouring countries from falling under communist influence. At the height of the Vietnam War there were around half a million US soldiers in Vietnam. The **guerrilla** forces of North Vietnam known as the **Viet Cong**, however, could not be defeated and the United States began to withdraw from South Vietnam. In 1975, the North Vietnamese army began a massive attack on the South. Within 3 weeks Saigon, the capital of South Vietnam, was under attack. US helicopters airlifted people out from the roof of the US embassy as the North Vietnamese army entered the city.

Helicopters evacuate people from the US embassy roof in Saigon, South Vietnam, as the North Vietnamese army engulfs the area.

South Africa

In South Africa, a minority of white people, about 9 per cent of the population, ruled over the majority of the population, 79 per cent of whom who were black. The white government ruled through a system of racist laws, called **apartheid**, but a black resistance movement had developed. In 1976, the government tried to impose Afrikaans, the language of the white people, in schools for black pupils. In Soweto, one of the very poor **townships** where black people in the cities were forced to live, demonstrations took place as a result. The police opened fire, killing around 200 people, and more demonstrations broke out around the country. Over the next 6 months, another 500 people were killed.

Rioters charge past the photographer as they protest against the compulsory teaching of Afrikaans in black schools in South Africa.

Leaving Vietnam, 29 April 1975

An Australian journalist witnessed US helicopters airlifting people from the US embassy in Saigon, South Vietnam:

"The helicopter could hold 50 people, but it lifted off with 70. The pilot's skill was breathtaking as he climbed to 60 metres [200 feet], with bullets pinging against the rotors [blades] . . . At least a thousand people were still inside the embassy, waiting to be evacuated . . . In the back of the helicopter there was a reminder of what we had left: a woman, whose daughter was still in Saigon, cried softly."

(FROM THE LAST DAY BY JOHN PILGER)

Superstars

In the United States, the charts were topped by disco music. This started off in discos in cities, but became more widely popular after the 1977 film *Saturday Night Fever*. Some of the most popular artists who recorded disco music were Abba, the Bee Gees, the Village People, and Gloria Gaynor. Disco music was typically made in studios with **synthesized** instruments. The exciting sound of disco sometimes lacked the live quality of rock music.

Disco fashion

In the UK, the outrageous clothes that disco stars wore became the current fashion. Performers such as Queen and Roxy Music wore extravagant clothes, and inspired fans to do the same. Women wore tight-fitting, shiny clothing and sky-high platform shoes, whilst men wore slim-fitting suits with oversized, pointed collars. The music itself was not one particular style and ranged from US-style disco to the **flamboyant** rock style of bands such as Queen.

Television

By the middle of the 1970s the format of most television shows was established. In the United States, long-running television series were planned to last an hour, allowing for advertisements, and told a complete story in each episode. In 1980, the popular *Hawaii 5 O*, a detective series set in Hawaii, came to an end. Two new series, *The 6 Million-Dollar Man* and *The Bionic Woman*, imagined a future where technology would be used to improve the skills of special agents. Another popular crime show from the period was *Charlie's Angels* and in the UK a comedy series, *Fawlty Towers*, began to be shown. Children's shows included *The Muppets*, *Sesame Street* and, in the UK, *Dr Who*. Long-running dramas with a continuing story, called soap operas, included *The Waltons* and *Little House on the Prairie*. Both shows celebrated a return to traditional family values. In the United States this was a popular reaction to Vietnam and economic recession.

These glamorous women starred in the popular American television series *Charlie's Angels*, about three female detectives who went undercover to solve crime.

Saturday Night Fever

The 1977 film *Saturday Night Fever* was about the disco culture of New York, United States. A working-class young man, Tony Manero, dedicates all his leisure time to preparing dance routines for disco-dancing competitions. In the course of the film, he moves away from the Brooklyn area into the more respectable neighbourhood of Manhattan.

The film made John Travolta an international film star. His typical dress style in the film, a slim figure wearing flared trousers and a tight white polyester jacket, became a familiar image of the 1970s.

John Travolta displays his famous disco pose from *Saturday Night Fever*, which became an instant dance-movie classic of 1977.

NEW DIRECTIONS

In the UK, Jubilee year 1977 celebrated the 25th anniversary of the Queens' inheritance of the throne. While some people arranged street parties and wanted to celebrate the event, other groups used it as an occasion to criticise the **monarchy**. The official opening of the National Theatre in London also started arguments. The theatre was criticised for the amount of money spent on it when theatres in smaller cities and towns could not afford to keep going. The economy began to improve, but the unemployment queues got no shorter.

Punk rock

A new style of rock music began to emerge in the 1970s, called punk rock. In Manhattan, New York, United States, bands such as the Ramones, the Dictators, Richard Hell, and the New York Dolls took the glam rock style of the early 1970s and gave it a harder edge, wearing torn clothes and wild hairstyles. In the United States, the music was a reaction to the pretentious trends of the rock bands that were popular at the time, such as Pink Floyd, or Fleetwood Mac. In the mid 1970s, a UK clothes shop owner called Malcolm McLaren visited New York and loved the style of the Ramones and the New York Dolls.

The Sex Pistols

Back in the UK, McLaren used what he had seen and heard in New York, and assembled and managed his own punk band, the Sex Pistols. In the three years that they stayed together, the Sex Pistols outraged many people. Their songs sounded angry and their lyrics were deliberately unromantic. Radio stations banned some of their songs. One banned song, "God Save the Queen," was about how the monarchy meant nothing to the angry youths that made up the punk movement. It was never played on the radio, but still reached number two in the UK music charts.

The Sex Pistols perform onstage, with Johnny Rotten as lead singer, in 1978.

Punks

Many punks belonged to a generation of young people who felt they had little to feel hopeful about. They criticised society, accusing it of being obsessed with money and **status symbols** such as fashionable cars and foreign holidays. While other teenagers wore platform boots and shiny clothes and went to discos, punks rejected mainstream fashion and made their own styles out of torn jeans, bin liners, old leather jackets with chains added, and safety pins through their ears. Their hair was formed into outrageous styles and punk girls wore make-up to shock rather than to make themselves look pretty.

Punk chic

It was not long before business-minded people found a way of making money from the growing interest in punk styles. UK dress designer, Zandra Rhodes, took elements of the punk style and used them to make more elegant clothes. She designed gold safety pins and jewelled chains, which made the outfits more acceptable to the rich and famous.

US punk rock group, the Ramones, wear leather jackets and torn jeans in a 1976 publicity shot.

The Clash

Formed in 1976, the Clash was another popular punk rock band. The Clash were more socially conscious and political than the Sex Pistols. Throughout their career in the 1970s and 1980s they tried not to be **exploited** by the big business of pop music. They always kept the prices of their records low, and many of their songs contained political messages. They toured with the Sex Pistols on their "Anarchy in the UK" tour in 1976. Most of the concerts were cancelled because The Sex Pistols had become so well known for behaving badly. In 1979, the Clash toured the United States and gained many fans there. Critics consider their 1979 album, *London Calling*, to be one of the most important albums in rock music.

The pace of life

In the decades before the 1970s, people had been gradually getting used to new inventions. They arrived slowly enough for people to learn to live with one new piece of technology before having to adapt to the next. By the late 1970s, however, new technology was being introduced into people's lives at an increasingly fast pace. One form of new technology that had entered people's lives was nuclear power – used to make electricity and to make weapons that were becoming more and more powerful. Some people began to see nuclear power as a threat as well as a benefit. While it gave clean, cheap electricity it was also capable of causing a lot of damage.

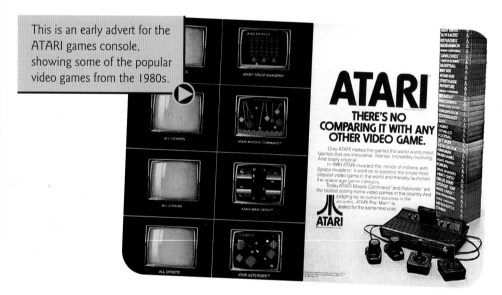

This is an early advert for the ATARI games console, showing some of the popular video games from the 1980s.

Advanced technology

By the middle of the 1970s, electronic calculators had become common. Video cassette recorders were quickly being developed and were set to become household items. Microwaves became affordable by the early 1980s. In 1972, a company called ATARI developed the first video games, which were at first played as coin-operated arcade games. ATARI had a hit with "Pong" (1972), while other companies went on to have success with "Space Invaders" (1978) and "Pac-Man" (1980). In 1972, the Magnavox Odyssey became the first at-home video game system. ATARI followed this with an at-home version of its own in 1977, and soon arcade games could be played on people's television screens. In 1985, Nintendo also introduced a popular home system. **Optical fibre** was quickly replacing electronic wires in telephone cables, making telephone systems more efficient. The very first cellular radio transmitters, the great grandparents of the mobile phone, were also being developed. In 1979, the Sony Walkman became the first portable cassette tape player to be produced.

Good news, bad news

In the early 1970s, scientists were working on methods of implanting **fertilized** human eggs into women who could not **conceive** babies naturally. In the UK, in 1978, the first child was born as a result of this method. Three years later, the same technology was used successfully in the United States.

In 1981, the first cases of what would later be identified as AIDS (acquired immune deficiency syndrome) were discovered in the United States – and in Australia two years later – although the cause of the disease was yet unknown.

Leisure technology

In the 1960s in California, United States, a small group of people began using narrow boards with wheels to travel along pavements (sidewalks). This became known as "sidewalk surfing", and soon evolved into skateboarding. Special parks were designed for skateboarders to perform stunts and compete with one another. By the early 1980s, the original simple skateboards had become more complex and skilled skateboarders had become stars amongst like-minded teenagers.

Another area where technology improved a popular sport was cycling. The bicycles of the 1960s were being replaced by new types such as BMX bikes. They were built for travelling at speed over rough ground, and for performing new stunts and tricks.

A young skateboarder shows off his daring stunts during the 1970s, when skateboarding became hugely popular.

Tony Alva

Born in 1957 in Santa Monica, Tony Alva became one of the first US superstars of skateboarding. At first he was a keen "sidewalk surfer" in the days when this was a very un-cool activity. By the late 1970s, skateboarding had become organized into a competitive sport and Tony was winning many of the competitions. He and the other Zephyr Boys (or "Z-boys") became famous skateboarders with their new, aggressive style of skating.

The pace in space

Throughout the 1970s both the United States and the USSR were spending a lot of time and money on space exploration. Unmanned space probes to other planets in the solar system were launched, and work began on space stations for scientific study and the training of astronauts.

Probes

In 1976, two US space probes landed successfully on Mars and launched robot landing vehicles that spent several years sending back data about conditions on the planet. In 1978, two Soviet probes landed on Venus and were able to analyse atmosphere samples before they burned up in the planet's temperatures of 460 degrees Celsius (860 degrees Fahrenheit). The USSR sent out more probes to Venus in 1981 and 1983. US orbiting probes mapped Venus in 1978. In 1977, two *Voyager* probes left the United States bound for Jupiter and Saturn. All this was made possible by the use of remote-controlled robotic equipment responding to radio signals sent out from Earth. The space probes and equipment were powered by **solar energy**.

Space stations

In this period, both the United States and USSR experimented with space stations. *Skylab* was launched by the United States in 1973. For 6 years it sent back information about the effects of long periods in space on the crews who manned it. It was destroyed in 1979 when an attempt to change its orbit around Earth caused it to fall back and burn up in Earth's atmosphere. The *Soviet Salyut 7* systems lasted for 9 years before falling out of orbit. They were used by crews from other nations including Cuba, France, and India.

Skylab, the US space station, which was launched in 1973, passes over the Earth during its 6-year orbit in space.

The shuttle

Most of the United States's spending on space travel during this period went towards developing a reusable spacecraft. By the time of its launch in 1981, *Columbia*, the first space shuttle, had cost US$10 billion. The shuttle was launched like a rocket with reusable rocket boosters falling away as their fuel was used up. It was designed as a service ship for satellites. It could carry materials up to existing satellites or it could repair or bring back broken ones. On its return to Earth the shuttle glided back into the atmosphere, its surface protected by heat resistant shields, and landed on a runway.

Columbia: facts and figures

The space shuttle *Columbia*:

- was made up of 2.5 million parts
- had 370 kilometres (230 miles) of wire and 27,000 insulating tiles
- was capable of travelling through temperatures ranging from −156.7 degrees Celsius (−3,000 degrees Fahrenheit) to 1,648 degrees Celsius (3,000 degrees Fahrenheit)
- at launching accelerated from zero to 28,000 kilometres (17,400 miles) per hour within 8.5 minutes, using 1.59 million kilograms (3.5 million pounds) of fuel to do so
- weighed 2.04 million kilograms (4.5 million pounds)
- had three main engines that produced 23 times more power than the Hoover Dam per minute.

(SOURCE: NASA)

The first space shuttle, *Columbia*, is launched in a cloud of smoke from Kennedy Space Center, Florida, United States, on 12 April 1981.

China after Mao

In 1976, Mao Zedong, China's leader for over 20 years, died. More than just a leader, Mao had planned and built a new society for China. He survived a challenge to his power by launching the Cultural Revolution in 1966. During this period Mao's young supporters, called the Red Guard, had wrecked factories and attacked people they thought were **reactionaries**. The lives of many innocent people were ruined as they were charged with being against the revolution and put on trial. Overall, though, Mao won tremendous respect from most people in China.

Power struggle

When Mao died, China was not very involved with the rest of the world. Although it had made great improvements in some areas of people's lives, such as education and food production, it was still behind the West in science and technology. When Mao died there was no system for putting a replacement leader in power and different groups fought for control of the country. One group was led by Deng Xiaoping – a man who wanted China to change its economy to become more like the West. Another group, known as the Gang of Four, were led by Mao's wife. They wanted to keep China the way it was and not make any changes. The Gang of Four were arrested in 1976 and by the end of 1978, Deng Xiaoping had gained the upper hand and emerged as China's new leader.

The Chinese Premier, Deng Xiaoping, and US President, Jimmy Carter, wave from the south balcony of the White House, Washington, D.C., United States, 29 January 1979.

Deng's policies

Deng realized that if China was to modernize it needed the help of the West. From 1978, China moved towards "market socialism." This was a form of communism, but it allowed parts of capitalism to exist. Deng took on loans from foreign governments and ordered modern equipment from the West for China's factories. At home he organized the return of land and property that had been taken from people during the Cultural Revolution. Government-owned farms and factories were allowed to plan their own work rather than follow the government plans. Taxes were lowered and people were allowed to make profits. Both the West and the Soviet Union watched to see what might unfold with a mixture of curiosity and scepticism.

Democracy Wall

In Peking (now called Beijing) people began putting posters up on a place known as **Democracy Wall**. At first Deng had approved because all the posters had criticised the rulers who went before him. Then the posters began to criticise him. There were demonstrations in Peking for more democracy. Deng suddenly clamped down on his critics, demolishing Democracy Wall in December 1979 and arresting people who disagreed with his policies.

Chinese people read the posters that were pinned up on the Democracy Wall in Peking, China, August 1979.

By the late 1970s the UK's economy was doing badly. The government had to rely on a huge loan from the International Monetary Fund (IMF). In August 1977, unemployment rose above 1.6 million and trade unions began to ask for higher wages. During the winter of 1978–1979 there were a number of strikes, with ambulance staff, dustmen, sewer workers, and hospital staff on strike over pay and working conditions. It came to be known as the "winter of discontent." In 1979, after a general election, the Conservative Margaret Thatcher became the UK's first woman Prime Minister.

Year Zero

During the Vietnam War, Cambodia had been bombed by the United States in the hope of preventing the Viet Cong from using the country to transport supplies into Vietnam. Previously a very peaceful country, Cambodian society was badly affected by the bombing. In 1975, the Cambodian government lost power and a new communist government was formed. Pol Pot was the leader of the new party that ruled Cambodia: the Khmer Rouge.

Year Zero was the name given to 1975 by the Khmer Rouge. The party planned a completely new society for Cambodia. The cities were emptied and people were driven into the countryside to help grow food. Schools, radio stations, and mail delivery – most normal aspects of city life – were destroyed and people were expected to live as **peasants**. Anyone thought to be against the government was executed. During the following 4 years over 1 million Cambodian citizens died from famine and as a result of the harsh policies of the Khmer Rouge.

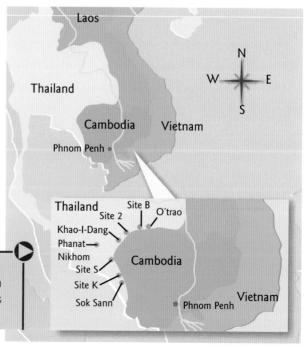

This map shows the Cambodian refugee camps in Thailand, which existed during the Khmer Rouge's leadership and for a decade after.

Vietnamese invade Cambodia

The Khmer Rouge came to think of Vietnamese people, many of whom lived in southern Cambodia, as its enemy and by 1977 the two countries were at war. China was sending aid to the Khmer Rouge, but by 1979 the Vietnamese were winning the war and they invaded Cambodia. The Khmer Rouge fled to Thailand. People were allowed to return to the cities, schools and monasteries (places where monks live) were reopened, and people began to build their lives again. The Khmer Rouge tried to take the country back and began an unsuccessful guerrilla war.

This is one of the refugee camps in Nong Samett, Thailand. Cambodians fled to these camps after Vietnamese troops invaded their country in 1979.

A closed world

Cambodia, renamed Kampuchea by the Khmer Rouge, closed itself off from the outside world. No foreigners were allowed into the country and no news was allowed to leave. Only Khmer people were seen as "pure" Cambodians and Vietnamese people living in the country were killed or sent out of the country. Few people outside of the region had any idea of the **genocide** that was taking place inside the country.

Alarm in Iran

In the 1970s, the Middle East, which contains about one third of the world's oil, was brought into the Cold War between the United States and USSR. Both superpowers wanted to make sure the other side did not have too much influence in the Middle East. Iran, one of the oil-rich countries, which also bordered on the USSR, had been friendly to the United States since 1953. The ruler of Iran, the Shah, had been helped to hold on to his power with the military and financial support of the United States.

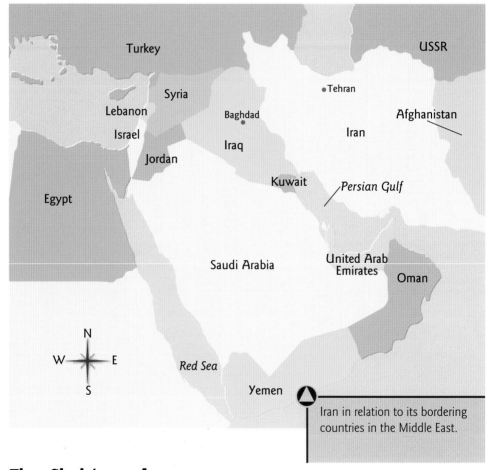

Iran in relation to its bordering countries in the Middle East.

The Shah's rule

Many people in Iran, a Muslim country, opposed the Shah. He was thought to be too friendly to the West and traditional religious leaders viewed this as suspicious. As a reaction against the Shah, they called instead for a return to the basic (fundamental) beliefs of **Islam**. For this reason they became known as **fundamentalists**. By 1978, they were strong enough to force the Shah from power. In 1979 he fled from Iran to Egypt.

Spreading alarm

Iran's new religious government was ruled over by the **Ayatollah** Khomeini. In November 1979, after the Shah had been allowed to enter the United States, the US embassy in Tehran, (Iran's capital), was attacked and 66 US hostages were taken. The Ayatollah threatened to put some of them on trial for **espionage**. After negotiations for their release failed, a rescue attempt was made. This went wrong, however, when a helicopter and refuelling aircraft collided, and eight US soldiers were killed. The failure to force Iran to release the hostages, as well as the failed attempt at rescue, had an enormous impact in the United States. Eventually, in 1981, the US hostages were released.

Iran-Iraq war

After the establishment of the new government in Iran, various groups began fighting for control. People disloyal to the new government were executed. In 1980, the neighbouring country of Iraq invaded Iran and captured valuable oil fields. The war between the two countries continued until 1988 when both sides, exhausted and unable to achieve victory, ended the fighting.

Demonstrators, angry at the Shah's friendship with the West, burn the United States flag at the US Embassy.

Ayatollah Ruhollah Khomeini

Many people supported Ruhollah Khomeini because they saw him as Iran's liberator. Born in a small desert town, he became a follower of an Islamic teacher and gradually became a leader of a Muslim **Shiite** group. As an opponent of the Shah's government, he spent the 1960s and 1970s in **exile** in Iraq. He returned in 1979 and became the country's leader in an Islamic revolution. This changed society completely, making it an Islamic republic and introducing Muslim law. In 1989, he called for the execution of a UK writer, Salman Rushdie, for publishing a book called *The Satanic Verses*, which he regarded as disrespectful to Islam.

Heat of the Cold War

Since the Second World War, the two superpowers, the United States and the USSR, had built up huge stockpiles of weapons – enough to destroy the entire world. Some people, such as the US and UK governments thought that this kept the world safe. They talked about Mutually Assured Destruction (MAD). The idea was that both the United States and the USSR knew that if either one started a nuclear war then both countries, along with the rest of the world, would be completely destroyed. This would happen, it was argued, because both sides had so many deadly weapons. So this kept either side from starting a war in the first place. Instead, a Cold War went on where the two sides never actually fought each other.

This nuclear missile, a weapon of mass destruction, rests on its missile launcher during the height of the Cold War, in 1980.

Afghanistan

In 1979, relations between the two superpowers grew troubled because of a war in Afghanistan. Groups there wanted to establish an Islamic government. In 1979, the USSR invaded Afghanistan and put a non-Islamic government in power. The USSR wanted to avoid the threat of Islamic uprisings in Soviet areas close to Afghanistan where many **suppressed** Muslims lived. Civil war broke out with all the other Afghan groups opposed to Soviet occupation. Fundamentalist groups were given weapons by the United States in order to fight and weaken the USSR. The Soviet army was unable to win and withdrew in 1989. Over 4 million **refugees** had fled from their Afghan villages into Pakistan.

Flight KAL007

On the night of 1 September 1983 a Korean passenger jumbo jet, Flight KAL007, flew into Soviet air space, apparently by accident. It ignored repeated warnings to leave and was shot down, killing everyone on board. This led to a serious heating up of the Cold War. The United States accused the USSR of **terrorism**. The USSR accused the United States of using the passenger plane as part of a spying mission. It is possible that the truth about Flight KAL007 will never be known.

The 1980 Olympic Games

One casualty of the new phase of the Cold War was the 1980 Olympic Games, due to be held in Moscow in the USSR. US President Jimmy Carter forced the US Olympic team to **boycott** the Olympics following the Soviet invasion of Afghanistan. Under pressure from their own governments, over 60 other countries followed. The UK did not withdraw as the Prime Minister Margaret Thatcher announced that governments had no right to interfere in sporting events. The Olympics took place but with very few competitors. Many athletes who had spent years preparing were unable to take part.

The opening ceremony of the 1980 Olympic Games, in Moscow, Russia, displayed huge symbols of communism, such as Lenin's image in the crowd.

THE AGE OF REAGAN

In the UK, years of economic decline between 1979 and 1983 were followed in 1984 by an economic boom. Margaret Thatcher's government believed that high government spending on medical care and education was bad for the country. People were encouraged to plan for themselves by taking out their own health insurance schemes and even by sending their children to private schools if they could afford it. The US President Reagan also held these views. Other people argued this attitude would only benefit the wealthy. The less wealthy, they argued, would receive second-class treatment in areas such as medical care.

New leaders

Jimmy Carter had been US President since 1977. As President he had signed agreements with the USSR and China and had helped bring about talks between Egypt and Israel. Carter had also been responsible, however, for the hostage rescue in Iran that went badly wrong (see pages 22–23). He lost popularity and was seen by many Americans as a weak leader. In 1981, Carter lost the election for president, after serving only one term, and Ronald Reagan became president.

Reagan

Ronald Reagan, a former film actor, was enormously popular as president. He called the USSR the "evil empire" and described the Cold War as a war between good and bad. It seemed to offer a simple explanation for world problems that were really very difficult.

Under President Reagan a new stage in the Cold War started. He began a large build-up of nuclear weapons. Countries in Europe friendly to the United States agreed to have them stored there in military bases, because their governments felt it would improve their security and because the United States was a powerful **ally** to have.

US President Ronald Reagan shows support for the Strategic Defence Initiative (SDI), also known as "Star Wars," in April 1987.

SDI
COULD RUIN A NUCLEAR BOMB'S WHOLE DAY.

Star Wars

In 1983, Reagan announced a new plan for US defence, called the Strategic Defence Initiative (SDI). This was a plan to put space stations in orbit that would guide laser guns based on Earth. These lasers would then be able to destroy any missiles targeted at the United States. It was nicknamed Star Wars, after the film, because it seemed far-fetched and futuristic to people who thought it would be a huge waste of money. The USSR took the plan seriously and called for it to be ended. For the first time in two decades all talks between the United States and the USSR stopped.

Star Wars: some facts

The SDI system, if it had worked, was intended to provide the United States with a system of stopping incoming missiles. The destroyed missiles would explode over the sea, away from US soil. The system would have included machinery in space and on the ground to detect the missiles and mirrors and lasers to guide the US defence system. The system would have cost somewhere between US$100 billion and US$1 trillion. The system was never actually developed.

This is an artist's interpretation of how the SDI system would have worked in space.

Troubled times

Around 1980, there were economic problems in the United States and Europe once more. Factories closed and unemployment began to rise. Many ordinary people took to the streets in protest. Also, the amount of taxes that governments could collect was less than before. This was because people had less money to spend.

Reaganomics

Some US economists claimed that there was a solution to these economic problems. Big industries, such as steel and car manufacturers, should reduce their numbers of workers and bring in computer-run machinery to do their work. This would save money. At the same time, businesses should be given tax reductions. This, it was argued, would encourage them to invest in industry that could then expand and take on new workers, who would work in administration rather than making the goods. People who were better off because of tax cuts would spend money on goods and this would improve the industries making these goods. Unemployment would fall again and the economy would grow stronger. Because the theory was put into operation during the presidency of Ronald Reagan, it came to be known as Reaganomics.

President Reagan began to put policies like these into practice. The immediate effect was to make things worse for the poor. Unemployment rose to 11 per cent. In some towns, where many people depended on one industry for work, there was very high unemployment.

Welcome banners await the People's March for Jobs, as the demonstrators reach London after 28 days walk from Liverpool, England, 28 May 1981.

Thatcherism

In the UK, under Prime Minister Thatcher, similar policies were adopted. By the end of 1979, unemployment was increasing. As in the United States, the worst hit were factory workers and young people looking for their first job and with no experience to offer employers. Middle-aged people who lost their jobs also found it hard to find new work. Some never returned to the workforce. In manufacturing, 2 million jobs were lost. The economists that advised Thatcher said this would be all for the best. There was no point, Thatcher agreed, in keeping industries going that would eventually go out of business. By 1983, 3 million people in the UK were unemployed – double the rate of 1979.

Northern Ireland

In 1981, trouble flared once again in Northern Ireland, where some people were campaigning for independence from the UK. In 1980, **nationalist** prisoners in the Maze prison outside Belfast were refusing to wear prison clothes on the grounds that they were political prisoners and not criminals. They wore only their blankets to cover them. Then, in 1981, several prisoners began a **hunger strike** to demand that they be treated as political prisoners. The government refused and ten men died of starvation.

This mural shows Bobby Sands, one of the prisoners who died following a 66-day hunger strike at Maze Prison, Belfast, Northern Ireland, on 5 May 1981.

More wars

The Falklands War

In April 1982, Argentina invaded the Falkland Islands, a UK **colony** in the South Atlantic, which they called Las Malvinas. The Argentineans captured the main settlement of Port Stanley. One reason for this might have been that oil exploration was going on in the area and they wanted any new oil deposits. The Argentine government was also unpopular at the time with the Argentinean people and may have used the invasion as a way of gaining support.

The sinking of the Argentinian ship, the *Belgrano*, during the Falklands War, makes front-page news on 10 May 1982.

A UK naval force set sail for the Falklands. It was a 2-week journey to the islands. In late April UK soldiers landed on South Georgia, the smaller of the two inhabited islands. A 322-kilometre (200-mile) **exclusion zone** was set up around the islands and any ship entering it was considered to be an enemy. In early May an Argentinean naval ship 48 kilometres (30 miles) outside the exclusion zone, and sailing away from the islands, was torpedoed by UK submarines. Hundreds of Argentinean crew died and this angered many people in the UK. By July 1982 the Falklands War was over. The Argentineans surrendered, and the UK Prime Minister Margaret Thatcher announced: "Great Britain is great again." General Galtieri, the Argentinean **dictator**, was removed from power. A thousand people had died in the war – 256 of them from the UK.

Public reaction to the war

Up until the fighting began the Falklands War had seemed unreal to most people in the UK. Some people were against the war, but many others supported it. Some newspapers stirred up **patriotic** feelings in support of the war. Before Argentina invaded the islands, Thatcher was losing public support as UK Prime Minister. There was trouble in Northern Ireland, unemployment was high, and riots had occurred in some UK cities. After Argentina's defeat, Thatcher's popularity increased a lot.

Massacre in Lebanon

In Lebanon, a **civil war** had been raging since 1975 between Christians and Muslims, and between rival Arab and Islamic groups. This conflict became part of the Cold War with the United States and the USSR supporting different sides in the fighting. The situation was made even more complicated because parts of southern Lebanon had been turned into refugee camps for Arab **Palestinian** people. From these camps Palestinian fighters launched attacks against Israel. They wanted Israel to withdraw from land occupied as a result of an earlier Arab-Israeli war in 1967.

In 1982, Israel invaded southern Lebanon. The idea was to stop Palestinian forces attacking Israel. In 1982, Israeli troops were ordered by the government to stand by and do nothing while a Lebanese group massacred hundreds of Palestinian **civilians**.

In 1983, 260 US marines were killed in a bomb attack by Islamic terrorists in Lebanon and this led to a withdrawal of US forces from the country.

A huge bomb explodes on the beachfront in Beirut during the Israeli attack on Lebanon in 1982.

Even more wars

Like the civil war in Lebanon, many of the wars of the 1980s were related, in different ways, to the larger Cold War conflict between the two superpowers, the United States and the USSR.

Nicaragua

Nicaragua, the largest country in Central America, was not a democracy where people voted for a government. It was a country ruled by a family who would not stand for any opposition – the Samozas. They grew very rich at the expense of ordinary Nicaraguans. By 1979, a civil war had broken out and the Samozas were overthrown by a group called the Sandinistas. A **socialist** government took power and set about improving life for Nicaraguans.

US President Reagan saw the Sandinistas as a threat because they did not support the United States. In 1981, the **US Congress** agreed to fund a rebel group called the Contras, who received arms and training from the United States. In 1984, the Contras organized the mining of the ports of Nicaragua. This caused damage to commercial ships belonging to other countries, many of which were allies of the United States, so Congress withdrew support for the Contras. A secret plan by the **White House**, however, continued to support the Contras. Funds from the secret sale of arms to Iran were given to the Contras to buy weapons. This became public knowledge in 1986. The man in charge of the operation, Oliver North, was held responsible and brought to trial. The revelations about the scandal seriously affected President Reagan's popularity.

Lieutenant Colonel Oliver North, of the US Marine Corps, is sworn in to testify for hearings on the Iran-Contra affair, 9 December 1986.

El Salvador

A similar situation developed in El Salvador. Here an **undemocratic** military force held power with the assistance of money and arms from the United States, who wanted to stop the communist opposition group from gaining power. The communists conducted a guerrilla war against the country's rulers. This civil war went on with neither side winning. Many thousands of people were killed as a result of government "death squads" and one in five of the population fled the country.

The United States supported the El Salvador government because, it was argued, if the communists won they would impose communism on South America and give support to the USSR in the Cold War. The same reason was given for supporting the Contras in Nicaragua. Critics of US foreign policy said that this was only an excuse. The real reason for supporting undemocratic governments in South America, critics said, was to stop socialist governments from democratically taking power in Central America. Such governments would not support US businesses, which were interested in developing new markets in South America.

Demonstrators march in San Salvador before the outbreak of civil war in El Salvador, 1979.

CULTURE AND CONFLICT

By the early 1980s, some new social patterns were emerging in the UK. More people were paying for private health care and private schools. Young professional people in some occupations were able to afford luxuries like more than one foreign holiday a year. These people became known as yuppies. Yuppie also became a term of criticism. Some people used the word yuppie to describe a lifestyle that was concerned only with spending money, displaying wealth and looking good.

Dance music

The world of popular music was changing. Elvis Presley died in 1977. In 1980, The Beatle's John Lennon was murdered in New York, United States. Lennon's senseless death shocked the world and upset many admirers of his music and ideas. By the 1980s, punk music was becoming less popular.

Clubland

By the early 1980s, disco music had also become unfashionable and in its place a new kind of music began to evolve. Emerging from the Chicago disco scene, it consisted of old disco tunes with remixes by club DJs. In 1983, the Muzic Box Club opened in Chicago and it is probably here that disco music evolved into house music.

Grandmaster Flash, shown here in 1981, was one of the pioneers of Hip-Hop DJing. He continues to DJ all over the world today.

The music was louder and faster than disco music and it used drum machines. It was music to dance to rather than performance music. The use of drugs became a common part of the house music scene.

By 1985, record companies such as Trax Records were recording house music, which allowed it to reach a wider audience. The music caught on in Europe and was played in clubs in the UK and Spanish holiday resorts. DJs associated with this music became well known and they toured clubs in the UK and rest of Europe. In the United States, however, house music remained a **cult** phenomenon.

In the United States, emerging out of house music came techno music, developed in Detroit by a group of African-American college students. They were inspired by the music of Kraftwerk and Tangerine Dream, and a late night radio show hosted by DJ Charles Johnson.

A break-dancer performs his acrobatic moves to the crowd in 1984.

Hip-Hop

Hip-Hop began in the 1970s when New York DJs, like Afrika Bambaataa and Kool Herc, started mixing Jamaican reggae with funk, disco and soul music. Friends of the DJs began speaking to the crowd in time to the music. First called MC's (masters of ceremonies), these friends later became known as rappers. By the 1980s, Hip-Hop had become popular in the United States and was becoming popular in the UK and Europe. Along with the music went:

- a style of dressing, based on tracksuits and trainers
- a form of art, seen in the graffiti of the subways and streets
- an energetic and acrobatic form of dancing called break-dancing.

Music videos and MTV

Music programmes on television began in the 1960s in the UK and caught on in the United States later. Usually bands were filmed miming to their songs, and these films could be played on live television shows if the band could not get there to perform live. By the middle of the 1970s most successful bands were making these videos. In August 1981, a US company launched a satellite channel called MTV (Music TV) that played these music videos as well as new videos from current artists 24 hours a day. This helped to increase the popularity of music videos.

Power Dressing

To match the new lifestyles of "yuppies," young people with well-paid jobs, a way of dressing appeared that reflected their sense of confidence. It became known as "power dressing" and described clothing for well-off professional people at their places of work. Power-dressed men and women wore suits, with wide padded shoulders. Skirts were knee length and straight. The effect on women's outlines was to make them look more **masculine**. The style of dressing for women probably reflected the fact that up until now, women rarely had high-paying, powerful jobs. They needed to convince the world and their employers that they were the equal of men.

Designer fashions

For the first time, clothes with the name of their designers displayed on them became fashionable. Chain stores owned by the designers opened up. It became fashionable for suit jackets to be worn casually with the sleeves rolled up. Large department stores began to reorganize their women's fashion departments, adding little **boutique**-like sections selling the clothes of just one designer.

Sports gear

Along with the fashion for smart clothes, and in order to look good at work, many young professionals became hooked on a craze for exercising. Going to the gym became a national pastime in Europe and the United States. Gyms also became places where fashion was important. Tracksuits with designer sport labels, worn previously only by athletes, became highly fashionable, along with trainers and leotards.

"Yuppies" enjoy the high-life of the 1980s.

Power dressing on television

Several US television shows became associated with this new lifestyle and way of dressing. *Dallas* and *Dynasty*, two shows about wealthy families, featured female characters wearing suits with padded shoulders and fashionably big hairstyles. *Miami Vice* would have been just another police drama, except that the lead characters, Crockett and Tubbs, were very trendy. Crockett and Tubbs became the coolest detectives in the world, drove cool cars, wore pastel designer jackets over simple T-shirts, and always had their sleeves rolled up.

New Romantics

Some young people developed a form of dressing called New Romantic. Popular performers such as Adam and the Ants, Prince, Culture Club, and Duran Duran took on this fashion. They looked flamboyant, with pirate costumes, lots of make-up, cloaks, hats, and soft materials such as silk and velvet.

The artist Prince, wearing a flamboyant costume typical of the New Romantics, plays guitar in a 1985 performance.

Designer art and architecture

In the 1980s, it became fashionable for well-off couples to enjoy expensive holidays in foreign locations and fill their homes with new **consumer goods**. Some people made fun of yuppies because what they owned seemed to be their way of telling friends and neighbours how successful they felt themselves to be. One aspect of this lifestyle was to buy and display at home the work of new, young artists.

This is a painting by the artist Jean-Michel Basquiat, simply named *Success*, from 1980.

Art of the 1980s

The US artist Julian Schnabel produced "plate paintings" using traditional materials, such as oil and canvas, mixed with broken pottery. It had a child-like look and became part of a US movement called neo-expressionism. In New York, another kind of painting became known as Graffiti Art because it developed from the graffiti that decorated the city's subway trains. Jean-Michel Basquiat painted pictures in this way. Other artists such as Jeff Koons assembled things like soft toys or ornaments from **popular culture** and displayed them in Perspex boxes.

The Menil Collection

In 1982, work began on new buildings to hold the collection of art works owned by Dominique de Menil. The buildings included an art gallery, and an arts space for music, theatre, and educational projects. The buildings were set in a small park and surrounded by low-rise residential housing. The design, while still very modern, reflected the local buildings, using traditional timbering on the outside walls. Like many high-tech buildings this one focused on getting as much natural light inside the building as possible.

Architecture

New forms of architecture used new materials and technology, like many of the new consumer goods on the market. Called "high tech," this architecture first arrived in the early 1970s in the form of the Pompidou Centre in Paris, designed by Richard Rogers and the Italian Renzo Piano. It was created to show its structural details on the outside, instead of the usual practice of hiding them behind the building's skin of brickwork. With the Pompidou Centre, the frame, the air-conditioning pipes, even the lifts and escalators were brightly painted and visible from the outside.

In London, the Lloyds Building – also designed by Richard Rogers – added more to high tech. Made from steel and polished concrete, the building also displays its structures on the outside. In the United States, the Menil Collection building in Houston Texas, designed by Renzo Piano, was a gentler use of the high-tech methods, blending into the surrounding low-rise houses, and using more traditional materials.

The Lloyd's Building in the City District of London, was designed by Richard Rogers and built between 1979 and 1984.

The most successful high-tech building is considered by many to be the Hong Kong and Shanghai Bank building in Hong Kong. Designed by Norman Foster, the entire 179-metre- (587-foot-) high building hangs from huge steel masts. The outer skin of the building is glass and, looking at it from the street, the workings of the building and its occupants can be seen.

Old fears revisited

During the 1980s, people began to have serious worries again about the dangers of nuclear weapons. A war involving some of these weapons seemed a very likely possibility and people wondered if anyone could survive a nuclear explosion.

Some newspapers in the United States and Europe began to carry advertisements for personal nuclear fallout shelters. In Europe, it seemed to many that in the event of nuclear war both the USSR and the United States would try to destroy the other side's missile sites before the missiles could be fired. Many of these missile sites were in Europe. Europe would be the first casualty in any nuclear war between the superpowers. Some Australians visiting Europe at that time began to joke that they wanted to see it while it was still there. An anti-nuclear movement gathered support, arguing that western Europe would only be safe if these nuclear weapons were removed.

This is a film still from the television drama *The Day After* (1983), which showed what life might be like after a nuclear attack.

Greenham Common

The United States had military bases around Europe where nuclear cruise missiles were kept, waiting to be used if the order was given. The anti-nuclear movement argued that if the USSR felt seriously threatened it would first attack these bases in order to try and destroy the weapons before they could be fired at them. One of these bases was at Greenham Common in the south of England.

The Greenham Common base was surrounded by common land, which meant the land was open to the public and could not be closed off. Around the outside fence of the base, groups of women protestors established protest camps. The women lived in tents, cooked on open fires, and depended on supplies brought to them by their supporters.

Protestors warm themselves by a camp fire at the nuclear base of Greenham Common, Berkshire, England, January 1983.

Embrace the base

The women of Greenham Common lived on the outskirts of the air base for 19 years, from 1981 until 2000, when the last of the nuclear weapons were removed. Each of the nine entrances to the base had its own camp, each one with a different philosophy – Violet Gate was a religious group, Red Gate was where the artists lived. A few hundred women lived at the camps full time supported by others who brought food and supplies. On several occasions thousands of women and their male friends came to the camps to help. One of these occasions was December 1982 when 30,000 people, mostly women, met at the base and formed a human chain around it in a publicity stunt called "Embrace the Base." In December 1983, 50,000 women came to the base and cut down sections of the chain link fence around it. Hundreds were arrested.

CONFLICTING SIGNS

By 1985, the UK was becoming a more divided society. Differences between the lives of the rich and the poor were becoming more obvious. There were divisions between those who believed that nuclear weapons were keeping the world safe and those who believed survival depended on the removal of such weapons. One half of the country supported Thatcher's government, while the other half felt her policies were disastrous. A generation of young people began to turn away from politics and seemed to be interested only in having a good time.

Good times

In the United States, by the mid 1980s, President Reagan's economic policies were working. The recession had ended and the number of unemployed fell by millions. Factories were expanding and the cost of living was stable. The United States began to experience the longest period of economic growth since the end of the Second World War.

The Los Angeles Olympics

The 1984 Olympic Games were held in Los Angeles and the event seemed to sum up the United State's new confidence and pride. For the first time, the Olympics were run as a private, profit-making business, with sponsorship from 30 different companies that got advertising space at the games. A US television company bought the rights to televise the games and made large profits as a result.

The USSR and its supporters did not attend the Los Angeles Olympics. They stayed away in revenge for the US boycott of the 1980 Moscow Olympics. With the USSR and East Germany not competing, this made it a lot easier for the United States to win a record number of gold medals – 83 in total.

The 1984 US elections

On the wave of enthusiasm that his policies had brought, Reagan was voted in for a second term as president in November 1984, winning 49 out of the 50 states of the United States. His opponent, Walter Mondale, had pointed out the huge spending on weapons and the failure of the government to deal with the poor. He had also offered as a **running mate** a woman, Geraldine Ferrarro, for the first time in US history. Jesse Jackson, the first African-American candidate in US history, failed to get nominated, but he too pointed to the increasing gap between the rich and the poor, many of whom were African Americans.

US President Ronald Reagan takes the podium in Dallas, Texas, during the 1984 Republican Convention. He was elected 40th President of the United States in November of 1984.

Ronald Reagan's opponent, Walter Mondale, waves to supporters with his running mate Geraldine Ferraro, during the 1984 Democratic National Convention.

Not-so-good times

Not everyone felt they were benefiting from the good times that others were enjoying. In the United States, while some people enjoyed a better standard of living, one in five people were worse off. While tax reductions had given the country's poorest families a benefit of US$20 a year, it was calculated that reductions in **social security** payments had reduced their income by US$410.

The UK's miners strike

Critics of Margaret Thatcher's government in the UK claimed that a similar development was taking place there. Some people were becoming better off than ever before, but others – including many young people – were facing a future of unemployment.

Like President Reagan, Margaret Thatcher was re-elected prime minister in 1983. During her second term of office a dispute with coal miners divided the country. Thatcher wanted to close down a number of coal mines saying they could not make a profit, but this was strongly resisted by the miners and their union. The mines were situated in parts of the country where there was already high unemployment and this added to the problem. Starting in 1984, miners went on strike. They did not want an increase in wages, just guarantees of future employment. It became a very bitter strike that lasted over a year. Eventually, the striking miners were defeated. The planned mine closures went ahead and thousands of miners lost their jobs.

UK police officers surround hundreds of striking coalminers in June 1984.

Trouble around the world

In October 1984, the Conservative Party conference was held in a hotel in Brighton. The IRA had placed a bomb in the hotel several weeks before, and this exploded during the conference. The explosion killed five people and came close to killing the prime minister and all the major politicians in the government.

In the war between Iran and Iraq, Iran began putting mines in the waters of the Persian Gulf in an effort to disrupt Iraqi trade, and **merchant ships** not involved in the conflict were destroyed. In India, the prime minister, Indira Gandhi, was **assassinated**. In Ethiopia, an estimated 900,000 people died of famine.

The exterior of the Grand Hotel, Brighton, England, was destroyed when an IRA bomb exploded on 12 October 1984.

"Born in the USA"

In 1984, US singer Bruce Springsteen had an enormous hit with his song "Born in the USA." It was a song about how unwelcoming the United States had been to the soldiers returning from the Vietnam War in 1975. The troops had not received the usual heroes welcome, as many US citizens had disagreed with the war and did not see the soldiers as heroes at all.

However, many people completely misunderstood what the song was trying to say, including Ronald Reagan. He asked to use the song for his 1984 election campaign, mistakenly seeing it as a triumphant celebration of being American, and an expression of pride in the United States' achievements.

Springsteen famously objected to Ronald Reagan's request to play the song on his campaign trail. However, "Born in the USA" is often mistaken as a patriotic anthem today.

A world without windows

In the ten years between 1975 and 1985, enormous advances were made in technology and design. Perhaps the most significant of these was the home or personal computer (PC). In 1975, computers were slow, expensive, and of little use in the home, but this all changed from the early 1980s.

Apple

Several companies produced computers and each had its own software, stored on floppy discs, so called because the discs were bendy. Computers had no hard drives so each programme had to be small enough to store on one floppy disc. Early computers required users to type in code in order for the computer to complete tasks, and so many people found them difficult to use. Two young programmers, Steve Jobs and Steve Wozniak, decided to make computers more user-friendly. In 1977, they completed the Apple II computer, which was easier to use. Then, in 1982, they released the Lisa computer, which used icons (pictures) on the screen that could be clicked on with a mouse. Apple's more affordable Macintosh computer, released in 1984, also used this technology, and it revolutionized personal computers.

Enter Microsoft

In 1980, a large US computer company, IBM, asked a small programming company called Microsoft to design a user-friendly system for their brand of PCs. Microsoft came up with a system called MS DOS, which was confusing as it did not use icons. In 1985, IBM and Microsoft produced a new system that used icons called Windows. This would become major competition for Apple.

This was a 1984 advert for the new Apple Macintosh computer.

In the 1970s, small groups of computer users in the United States were linking their computers using telephone lines. The system was funded by the government and was not available to most people. In the early 1980s, this network system was extended to universities and some businesses. It was not yet called the Internet, and it was not well known, but it was the beginning of something very new and very powerful.

The first computer virus

Rich Skrenta – a 15-year-old boy from the United States – wrote the first computer virus in 1982 to annoy his friends. The virus was written on to a floppy disc and copied itself on to MS DOS, the computer's operating system. When a new programme was used, the virus copied itself on to the floppy disc and in this way travelled from one computer to another. The virus caused a poem to appear on the screen of the computer monitor:

"Elk Cloner: The programme with
    a personality
It will get on all your disks
It will infiltrate your chips
Yes it's Cloner!

It will stick to you like glue
It will modify ram too
Send in the Cloner!"

Another computer hacker, Robert Morris, sits at his computer. The American university graduate unleashed an Internet virus in 1988, which infected thousands of computers.

Perestroika

In December 1984, the deputy leader of the Communist Party that governed the USSR, Mikhail Gorbachev, made an important speech. He said there was a need for glasnost, a Russian word that meant the opposite of secret. It was translated as "openness." He wanted there to be more freedom of speech and more freedom to act in the USSR. Perestroika, he said, was also needed. This means: "changing the structure of something." He intended to allow some elements of **capitalism** into the Soviet economy, just as China was doing.

Gorbachev was telling the people of the USSR that life was going to change. The tight control that the Soviet government had over its people was going to be relaxed. The economic system was going to become more flexible, and people would be allowed to change its structure.

The following year, Gorbachev became the leader of the USSR. He began to change Russian society and, in doing so, change the whole world.

Ending the Cold War

Gorbachev knew that the standard of living for citizens of the USSR was poor compared to citizens of the West. Not enough goods were being produced or exported and the system was too slow to change. One main cause of the problem was that huge sums of money were being spent developing and maintaining nuclear weapons. An arms race – building bigger and more destructive nuclear weapons – was part of the Cold War. The USSR was in danger of **bankrupting** itself.

Gorbachev decided that the solution to the USSR's problem was to end the Cold War. The USSR did not want a war with the United States so why, he argued, waste huge amounts of money on weapons that would not be used? It would be better, he said, to spend the money on improving the Soviet economy. This would make people happier and help preserve the communist system.

President Ronald Reagan and the Soviet leader Mikhail Gorbachev are shown in one of their first meetings to discuss the removal of nuclear weapons from Europe, 21 November 1985.

The end of an era

Punk music arrived on the scene around 1975, and perestroika arrived ten years later. Punk was an expression of anger, disappointment, and boredom by young people who wanted the world to be a different kind of place. Perestroika was an expression of hope by a middle-aged man who thought that the world could be a different kind of place. The year 1985 was an important time in history as the world stood on the brink of a new relationship between East and West.

Steven Spielberg's 1983 movie, *ET*, was about an alien's unexpected friendship with a young boy. It seemed to mimic and predict the unexpected friendship that was developing between the Cold War superpowers by 1985.

Other events of the early 1980s:

- in 1983, the Ash Wednesday bush fires around Victoria, Australia, kill over 70 people
- in 1984, in Bhopal, India, a gas leak at a US-owned chemical plant kills 200 people and injures 200,000
- in 1984, in California, a fortnight-old baby with a serious heart defect is given the heart of a baboon. She dies twenty days later.
- in 1984, Svetlana Savitskaya and Kathryn D. Sullivan become the first women to walk in space.

TIMELINE

1972
ATARI develop first video games to be
played on coin-operated machines

1973
US space station *Skylab* is launched
The UK joins the European Union

1975
Recession in the West
Release of the film *Jaws*
North Vietnamese army enters Saigon
Year Zero in Cambodia
Civil War in Lebanon
Queen produce a music video for
their song "Bohemian Rhapsody"
Malcolm McLaren visits New York
and discovers punk rock there

1976
Riots in Soweto, South Africa
Death of Mao Zedong
Sex Pistols "Anarchy in the UK" tour
Two US space probes reach Mars

1977
Release of the film *Star Wars*
Release of the film *Saturday
Night Fever*
Queen Elizabeth II's Silver Jubilee
Concorde lands at JFK Airport
War between Cambodia and Vietnam
Jimmy Carter becomes president of
the United States
Elvis Presley dies
Two US *Voyager* probes set out for
Jupiter and Saturn

1978
The first test tube baby is born
Two Soviet space probes reach Venus
US orbiter satellite reaches Venus
"Space Invaders" home video game
is realeased
Chinese leader Deng Xiaoping
announces market socialism

1979
Skylab crashes to Earth and burns up
in atmosphere
Margaret Thatcher becomes prime
minister
The UK's "winter of discontent"
The Shah flees from Iran
US embassy in Tehran is attacked
and 66 hostages taken
USSR invades Afghanistan
Unemployment in the UK as high as
in the 1930s
A left-wing government comes to
power in Nicaragua

1980
Iraq invades Iran
Moscow Olympics boycotted over
Soviet invasion of Afghanistan
Recession in the West
Protests in Northern Ireland
John Lennon is killed
Microsoft invents MS DOS

1981

The first cases of AIDS are identified
  in the United States
The space shuttle *Columbia* is
  launched
Ronald Reagan is elected President
Dance music becomes fashionable
Hunger strikers die in jail in Belfast
US Congress votes funds for the
  Contra rebels in Nicaragua
MTV is launched
A Soviet space probe reaches Venus

1982

Argentina invades the Falkland Islands
Massacre of Palestinian refugees in
  Lebanon
The first computer virus is written by
  Rich Skrenta
Israel invades southern Lebanon

1983

Korean airliner shot down over the
  USSR's air space
A Soviet space probe reaches Venus
President Reagan announces the
  "Star Wars" initiative
Sally Ride becomes the first US
  woman in space
260 US Marines killed by Islamic
  terrorists in Lebanon
Muzic Box Club opens in Chicago
  in the United States

1984

The USSR and its **allies** boycott the
  Los Angeles Olympic Games
Bruce Springsteen releases "Born in
  the USA"
The year-long miner's strike takes
  place in the UK
Gorbachev declares a new era of
  perestroika
Mrs Gandhi is assassinated

1985

Gorbachev becomes General
  Secretary of USSR

1986

The Iran-Contra scandal is revealed

1989

Death of the Ayatollah Khomeini

FURTHER INFORMATION

CDs

Eyewitness: the 1970s (BBC Audiobooks, 2005)

Books

International Space Station: A Space Mission, Michael D. Cole (Enslow, 1999)

Internet Biographies: Bill Gates, Craig Peters (Enslow, 2003)

Nasa Planetary Spacecraft: Galileo, Magellan, Pathfinder, and Voyager, Carmen Bredeson (Enslow, 2000)

Rap and Hip-Hop: The Voice of a Generation, Sherry Ayazi-Hashjin (Rosen, 1999)

20th Century Fashion: The '70s: Punks, Glam Rockers and New Romantics, Sarah Gilmour (Heinemann Library, 2000)

20th Century Fashion: The '80s: Power Dressing to Sportswear, Claire Lomas (Heinemann Library, 2000)

20th Century Media: The 1970s and 1980s: The Global Jukebox, Steve Parker (Heinemann Library, 2003)

20th Century Science & Technology: 1970–90: Computers and Chips, Steve Parker (Heinemann Library, 2001)

Witness to History: Apartheid in South Africa, David Downing (Heinemann Library, 2004)

Websites

http://en.wikipedia.org/wiki/1900s
Wikipedia encyclopedia with sections on the 1970s and the 1980s.

www.geocities.com/historygateway/1900.html
Weblinks to interesting sites relevant to the history of women in the UK.

http://kclibrary.nhmccd.edu/decades.html
A history site dedicated to US cultural history on a decade-by-decade basis.

Disclaimer

All the internet addresses (URLs) given in this book were valid at the time of going to press. However, due to the dynamic nature of the Internet, some addresses may have changed, or sites may have ceased to exist since publication. While the author and publishers regret any inconvenience this may cause readers, no responsibility for any such changes can be accepted by either the author or the publishers.

the mid 1970s to the mid 1980s

Books and literature	• *The Silmarillion* by J.R.R.Tolkien/Christopher Tolkien (1977) • *The Bourne Identity* by Robert Ludlum (1980) • *Jumanji* by Chris Van Allsburg (1982)
Fads and fashions	• Cabbage Patch Kids, dolls with a unique birth certificate, become popular in 1983 • Rubik's Cube sells millions in the early 1980s, becoming an icon of the decade
Historic events	• Louise Brown, the first test tube baby, is born in the UK in 1978 • More women enrol for a college education than men for the first time in 1979, in the United States
Music, film, and theatre	• A combination of new technologies, such as Dolby sound, Panavision, and special effects, mean movies such as *Star Wars* and *Close Encounters of the Third Kind* are massive box office hits
People	• Chairman Mao Zedong, leader of the Republic of China, dies in 1976 • Michael Jackson has the best-selling album of all time with *Thriller* (1982)

GLOSSARY

ally people or a group who are on your side

apartheid system of racial discrimination enforced in South Africa by white-only governments until 1994

assassinate to deliberately target and kill someone

Ayatollah Muslim religious leader

bankrupting losing all their money

boutique small shop selling fashionable clothes

boycott refuse to take part in some event as a form of protest

capitalism economic system based on private ownership and profit

civilian non-military citizen

civil war war between groups within a country, not a war against another country

Cold War period of hostility between the United States and USSR that existed from 1945 until the late 1980s

colony country ruled over by another country

communist someone who believes in government ownership and spreading wealth

conceive become pregnant

consumer goods goods and products for everyday living

coronation ceremony where a king or queen is officially given their crown

cult popular amongst a group of people

democracy government where people of the country choose their leaders by voting for them

developing countries countries with low rates of economic growth

dictator non-democratic ruler who controls the government

economy matters relating to money

economic recession period during which trade and industrial activity reduce, and a country generates less wealth

empire control of other countries by a dominant country

espionage spying, to get information about another country's secrets

exclusion zone area set up by one group where members of other groups are forbidden to enter

exile when someone is forced to leave their own country and live in another one

exploited treat unfairly

fertilized made fertile, capable of living as a life form

flamboyant lively and bright

fundamentalist religious group who holds very strong views on morality and customs

genocide deliberate and organized killing of a group of people with the intention of destroying their identity as an ethnic, cultural, or religious group

guerrilla form of fighting against larger and more powerful forces which avoids an open battle

hunger strike deliberately going without food as a political protest

inflation when prices and wages are rising without any increase in production

IRA Irish Republican Army, a military group opposed to British rule in Northern Ireland

Islam religion of Muslims

masculine having male qualities

merchant ship boat carrying cargo to sell

Middle East mostly Arab countries located between Europe and Asia

monarchy political system with a king or queen as the highest representative

Muslim people who practise Islam

nationalist people with a strong belief in the value of their country

natural resources sources of energy found naturally, like gas or oil

optical fibre thin fibre that can carry light along its length

Palestinian people of Palestine, presently under control of Israel

patriotic strongly supporting one's own country

peasant person who works on the land

popular culture customs and traditions of ordinary people

reactionary someone who dislikes change and wants to go back to the way things were before a change

recession time when factories and businesses are closing and lots of people lose their jobs

refugee person who has no home

running mate person who stands for election as vice president in the US presidential elections

Shiite Muslim religious group

socialist someone who believes in a society that shares profit

social security government assistance for the needy

solar energy energy from the Sun

species group to which things belong because of shared resemblances

status symbol possession that shows someones wealth

superpower very powerful country with a lot of influence, like the United States and USSR during the Cold War

suppressed put down in a forceable way

synthesized artificially made

terrorism using violence and threats to try and make political changes

township specially selected urban areas where black people were forced to live under apartheid in South Africa

trade union organization formed by workers to protect their interests

undemocratic not part of a system of government where all citizens have the right to vote for their government

US Congress part of the law-making body of the United States

USSR Union of Soviet Socialist Republics

Viet Cong military Vietnamese force fighting US troops during the Vietnam War

West term referring to the way of life and government in Europe and North America

White House centre of government in the United States

INDEX

Titles in the *Modern Eras Uncovered* series include:

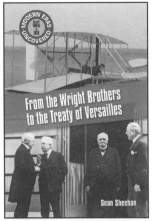

Hardback   1 844 43950 X

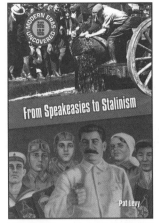

Hardback   1 844 43951 8

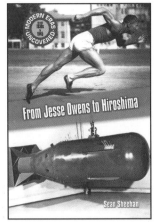

Hardback   1 844 43952 6

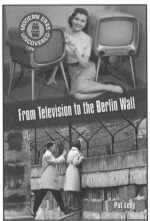

Hardback   1 844 43953 4

Hardback   1 844 43955 0

Hardback   1 844 43956 9

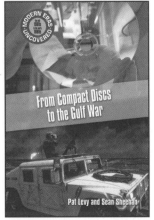

Hardback   1 844 43957 7

Hardback   1 844 43958 5

Find out about the other titles in this series on our website www.raintreepublishers.co.uk